lavender

figs

olives

herbs

citrus

walnuts

fennel

kale

tomatoes

farm fresh eggs

...a taste of Ojai

A Taste of Ojai

A Taste of Ojai

A COLLECTION OF SMALL PLATES

by Chef *Robin Goldstein*

Photographs by Karen Nedivi

Published by

PRIVATE CHEF ROBIN

Copyright © 2015 by Robin Goldstein

Printed in the United States of America

First Printing, 2015

ISBN: 978-1508863113

Printed through CreateSpace

• • •

Designed and produced by Tracy Smith Studio

www.tracysmithstudio.com

• • •

www.ATasteofOjai.com

www.privatechefrobin.com

Dedication

This cookbook is an homage to my Grandma Hilda,
the art of cooking she instilled in me as a young
child, is still a strong presence within me.

Table of Contents

Small Plates

Table of Contents

Introduction

Having exchanged my catering career for this diverse paced personal chef profession, my private clients, who know me as Private Chef Robin, have played an important role in the expansion of my culinary repertoire. Influenced by my travels and creating interesting foods with many plant based recipes, these 'small plates' highlight flavors reminiscent of the Mediterranean.

A great little collection of 'small plates', simple to sophisticated celebrating some of the harvests that grow plentifully right here in the Ojai Valley. Small and usually shared dishes based on foods I have tasted, Tapas in Spain, Mezze, in both Turkey and Greece, Italian Antipasti, as well as Moroccan and Middle Eastern dishes, with the emphasis on savory spice.

The thought behind this book is to present some ideas of foods that can be served as small plates for any time of day, just one plate or a collection of a few.

Cooking for me is an art, a flowy kind of natural rhythm I get into, not unlike driving or painting. I get into the moment and stop thinking, I just do. It feels so natural for me, it's in my blood. The first time I make a dish, I may be merely obeying a recipe, counting off the minutes until the sauce has simmered. After 30+ years, now I don't need the timer – I've learned how to smell the caramelized sugar of cooked onions, how to see when the bread is baked through... The dish is the same but my sense of it has become much richer.

My passion for cooking is driven by my desire to please and excite the palate, to see the joy in people's eyes and hear the mmm's when they taste...this is the pleasure I get on a daily basis and then, I am truly gratified.

"I believe that preparing food is about great ingredients, and it's about everything that goes into making a great meal. For me it's about sourcing well grown, local organic vegetables, the time I set aside to prepare a great dish, the music playing in the background, the tools I use in the kitchen, the vintage server and the beautiful plates I have collected over the years. It's about community and closeness and sitting at the table and enjoying the meal together with thanks."

with gratitude, Chef Robin

Lavender
French Grey Sea Salt
with Organic Lavender

FLAVORS WELL WITH:

Risotto, Rice

Chicken, Lamb, Cheeses

Pink Moment
Himalayan Pink Salt
with Pink Peppercorns

FLAVORS WELL WITH:

Seafood, Light Sauces

Set Jar on Table

Wild Fennel
French Grey Sea Salt
with Fennel

FLAVORS WELL WITH:

Eggs, Potatoes, Soups

Fish, Bloody Mary

Flavoring with Salt

Adding infused salt will elevate other flavors in your food, adding unique seasoning that shifts the taste ever so slightly. Throughout the book, in my recipes, you will notice that I refer to three variations of salt. Through much product research and testing, I found that these three distinct flavors enhance the Mediterranean influenced dishes so well, I have created in small batches and hand blend myself. Many of my recipes use these salts, feel free to experiment with different flavors you create yourself.

CULINARY
SEA SALT
Lavender
French Grey Sea Salt
with Organic Lavender

CULINARY
SEA SALT
Pink Moment
Himalayan Pink Salt
with Pink Peppercorns

CULINARY
SEA SALT
Wild Fennel
French Grey Sea Salt
with Fennel

Lavender's distinct aroma and flavor are instantly recognizable, which makes it a perfect unexpected culinary herb. With hand-picked organic herb's, adding this lavender infused salt will elevate other flavors in your dish imparting both a salty flavor and an herbal essence.

Lavender sea salt is exceptional in both chicken and fish dishes, and is a welcome addition in my Fig & Olive Tapenade and my handmade Lavender Fig Crackers and Lavender Mascarpone Spread. Season your favorite risotto or rice dish, marinate chicken and lamb, add to salad dressings to bring an incredible spring feeling to your meal.

Infused with lightly crushed hand-picked pink peppercorns, this pink salt pairs well with fish, seafood and in light sauces and dressings. Use at the table to add a pinch of light salt & pepper taste. Welcoming the many claimed benefits of this form of salt, such as reducing signs of aging, stronger bones, and improved sinus health, Himalayan Sea Salt contains the same 84 natural minerals and elements found in the human body and is famed to have zero exposure to toxins and impurities.

This coarse fennel sea salt infused with both organic wild fennel pollen and ground roasted fennel seed also has a very distinctive flavor. With quality ingredients, adding this fennel salt can elevate other flavors to your foods, imparting both a salty flavor and a fennel essence. Fennel works well with eggs and potatoes, in soups and broths, in my onion-fennel fritter recipe and is amazing in a Bloody Mary.

....

Tip: Get the ready-made versions of *A Taste of Ojai Culinary Sea Salt*, online at: www.atasteofojai.com

Small Plates

Pear Tartine

What we call "toast" the French call a "Tartine" which literally means "a slice of bread". Our sandwiches tend to be stuffed full between two slices of cut bread, in France their sandwiches are served open-faced using fresh and seasonal ingredients. Tartines can start the day with little more than butter and honey or jam. They can be a light lunch alongside an arugula salad and in the evening they can start the meal as an effortless appetizer. I like them because you can put anything you want on a piece of toasted bread and call it "Tartine" and suddenly it sounds so much more lovely and sophisticated than toast. SERVES 4

what you need

1 baguette

¼ cup olive oil

2 pears, thinly sliced

1 cup Lavender Mascarpone Spread
    see recipe on page 82) or 6 ounces
    French goat cheese

A Taste of Ojai Lavender Sea Salt
or your favorite sea salt

freshly ground pepper

how to make it

Preheat a stovetop grill on high.

Slice the baguette diagonally into ¼-inch slices. You should have 20 to 25 slices that are perfect for hors d'oeuvres. Brush each slice with olive oil. (You can cut the baguette lengthwise and then into 8 pieces to create larger portions). Brush the pear slices with a little olive oil. Lower heat to medium and first grill bread slices until lightly charred and toasty. Remove and then grill pears for 1 to 2 minutes on each side until lightly charred as well.

To serve, arrange the toasted bread on a baking sheet.

Spread each piece with Lavender Mascarpone spread and arrange the grilled pear slices to slightly overlap each other. Season with *A Taste of Ojai Lavender Sea Salt* and pepper. Serve on a wood board with your favorite marmalade, a drizzle of local honey, or my Balsamic Jam (see recipe on page 75).

Kale Polpettes

The translation of the Italian word **polpettes**—pronounced "pohl-PET-tahs," is "balls" or "dumplings"—but it's basically a fancy way of saying meatballs. These, however, are delightful, delicious meatless bites to be served as appetizers or a light first course with a baby arugula salad, sautéed vegetables, or tossed into pasta. MAKES ABOUT 30

what you need

1 pound potatoes, peeled

2 cups packed fresh kale

6 ounces fresh baby spinach

2 tablespoons salted butter

2 tablespoons extra-virgin olive oil, plus extra for cooking

1 small yellow onion, chopped

1 green onion, sliced thin

1 tablespoon nutritional yeast

1 teaspoon sea salt

1 teaspoon freshly ground pepper

2 cloves garlic, peeled and minced

½ teaspoon oregano

2 tablespoons soy milk

2 tablespoons potato starch or cornstarch

how to make it

Cut potatoes into ½-inch cubes and put into a medium pot filled with cold water just to cover. Bring to a boil and cook until potatoes are tender, about 8 to 10 minutes.

While the potatoes are boiling, remove the center stalk from the kale, discard, and slice the leaves into strips. When potatoes are tender, lift them out of water with a slotted spoon and drain in a colander to cool. Put the sliced kale leaves into the hot potato water and steam for 4 minutes or until kale is tender. Remove kale with a slotted spoon and drain in colander to cool. Put the spinach in the hot potato water and steam for about 2 minutes. Remove spinach with a slotted spoon, drain, and cool. Once kale and spinach has cooled down, squeeze out liquid from the greens.

Heat a small sauté pan and melt butter with olive oil. Add yellow onion and sauté until softened and translucent, about 5 minutes.

Preheat oven to 425°F and line a baking sheet with parchment, brushed with olive oil.

Put cooled potatoes, kale, spinach, and sautéed onions into the bowl of a food processor and pulse to chop fine, but do not puree. Add sliced green onions, nutritional yeast, salt, pepper, minced garlic, oregano, soy milk and cornstarch. Pulse a few times just to combine. It should be generously seasoned and taste a little bit salty and mixture should hold together to form a ball. if the mixture is too wet, add a touch more potato starch or cornstarch.

Using a well-rounded tablespoon or small scoop, form the mixture into 1-inch balls. Place them on the baking sheet and bake for 15 minutes. Carefully turn them over and bake for another 15 minutes, until lightly browned.

Baked Sweet Potato Falafel

Years ago on my first visit to the Middle East, I dined on falafel, which is typically made from fava beans or chickpeas and is popular among vegans and vegetarians. That sparked me to create my own version for a mezze platter, adding sweet potato for a healthful twist. Instead of frying it, I bake the falafel, drizzling it with olive oil to achieve that crispy, crunchy bite. MAKES 3 DOZEN BALLS

what you need

2 large sweet potatoes

1 cup cooked garbanzo beans, mashed

3 garlic cloves, minced

1 tablespoon fresh lemon juice

1 tablespoon Bragg Liquid Aminos or tamari sauce

2 teaspoons ground cumin seed

2 teaspoons ground coriander

1 teaspoon smoked paprika

¼ teaspoon cayenne pepper

1 teaspoon of *A Taste of Ojai Wild Fennel Sea Salt* or your favorite sea salt

½ teaspoon freshly ground pepper

½ cup fresh parsley, roughly chopped

½ cup fresh cilantro, roughly chopped

1 red onion, finely minced

½ cup garbanzo bean flour

2 tablespoons sesame seeds

olive oil, for baking

how to make it

Preheat oven to 400°F. Bake sweet potatoes for 1 hour or until they can be easily pierced with a fork. Cool completely. Peel and discard skins and put flesh into a medium bowl.

(Alternatively, you can boil 2 large sweet potatoes until tender, about 15 to 20 minutes.)

Mash potatoes with a fork. Add mashed garbanzo beans, garlic, lemon juice, Braggs, all spices, salt, pepper, parsley, cilantro, and red onion.

Continue to mash and add garbanzo bean flour until combined well and still a bit chunky in texture. Generously brush a baking sheet with olive oil. Scoop 1 tablespoon of mixture and form mixture into small balls using wet hands and place on the baking sheet. They can be close together as they do not expand while baking. Sprinkle with sesame seeds. Chill falafel balls in the refrigerator for about 1 hour.

Reduce oven temperature to 375°F. (If you prefer to make falafel patties to stuff into pitas, flatten them with a fork.) Drizzle falafel balls with more olive oil just before baking for 30 minutes until crisp.

Serve with tahini sauce as a small bite for an appetizer, or I like to crumble over a green salad with extra tahini sauce for dressing. They are also perfect in pita pockets with cucumbers, tomato, hummus and tahini sauce.

Lemon Tahini

The tahini we see in a jar is not ready to eat—it's not seasoned yet.

In a small bowl, add about ½ cup of tahini paste and 3 or 4 tablespoons of warm water; blend with a fork until it is smooth. Add the juice of ½ a lemon, more if you like it extra lemony as we do. Season with salt to taste and adjust the consistency with a little more water as needed. Add any of the following for extra flavor: fresh chopped garlic or organic garlic powder, chopped parsley, chopped cilantro, cayenne pepper, or even a hard-boiled egg—its OMG delicious!

Cauliflower Fritti

Fried cauliflower is an indulgence, but this crispy, lemony version is worth making—and eating. The addition of aromatic sofrito in this not-too-heavy chickpea batter make these mouth-watering morsels.   MAKES 4 SERVINGS

what you need

2 cups garbanzo bean flour

2 tablespoons cornstarch

2 cups cold water

3 tablespoons sofrito (see recipe page 89)

1 tablespoon of *A Taste of Ojai Wild Fennel Salt* or your favorite sea salt

1 teaspoon freshly ground pepper

1 tablespoon lemon zest from 1 lemon, and cut into wedges for garnish

1 teaspoon Spanish pimentón (smoked paprika)

1 head cauliflower, cut into medium-size florets

vegetable oil, for frying

how to make it

In a medium bowl, mix the garbanzo bean flour and cornstarch, then slowly mix in cold water, so it has the same consistency as pancake batter. (You may use a little less water than called for.) Add the sofrito, salt, pepper, lemon zest, and pimentón to the batter.

In a skillet over medium heat, add about 2 inches of vegetable oil. Use a thermometer to gauge the temperature, which should hover between 345°F and 350°F.

Dunk 8 to 10 cauliflower florets in the batter with your fingers. Before putting each floret in the skillet, shake off any runny batter, then drop each carefully into the hot oil. Don't overcrowd—this way the cauliflower will soften a bit and the batter will be crunchy.

Fry until golden brown on all sides, gently stirring with a metal spatula to turn over the pieces. It will take a few minutes per batch. Using a mesh strainer, scoop them out and drain on paper towels.

Sprinkle with another pinch of *A Taste of Ojai Wild Fennel Sea Salt*. Serve on a tray with fresh lemon wedges.

....

Tip: These are great eaten plain but even better when served with a flavorful creamy dip of equal parts mayo and dijon mustard seasoned with salt and pepper and a squeeze of fresh lemon juice.

Roasted Vegetable Crostata

This crostata is a great first course, for brunch or lunch and the mini's can be served as an appetizer. Try with my spicy tomato jam (page 81), for a kick. SERVES 6-8

what you need

FOR THE PASTRY:

1½ cups all-purpose flour

¼ teaspoon kosher salt

¼ pound (1 stick) very cold unsalted butter, diced

2-3 tablespoons ice water

FOR THE FILLING:

2 cups Vegetables, cut into 1" pieces

zucchini, asparagus, onions, tomatoes, peppers or what you have on hand

4 oz. goat cheese optional

6 farm fresh eggs

½ teaspoon salt

freshly ground pepper

how to make it

FOR THE PASTRY: Place the flour, salt and the butter in the bowl of a food processor fitted with the blade. Pulse a few times to combine until the butter is the size of peas. With the motor running, add the ice water all at once through the feed tube. Keep hitting the pulse button to combine, but stop the machine just before the dough becomes a solid mass. Turn the dough onto a well-floured board and form into a disk. Wrap with plastic wrap and refrigerate for at least 1 hour.

FOR THE CROSTATA: Preheat the oven to 425 F. For one 10" fluted tart pan or 12 cup mini muffin tin.

While dough is chilling, roast the vegetables.

Toss the cut vegetables in a little olive oil and salt and pepper. Roast on a baking pan for 30 minutes. Remove from oven and allow to cool.

While the vegetables are roasting, roll out the dough. On a lightly floured surface, roll the pastry into a 12-inch circle. Transfer the dough to the tart pan (or mini tart pans) and press it in. Chill for 30 minutes.

Arrange the cool roasted vegetables onto the chilled tart dough. Whisk the eggs with the salt and pepper and pour over the vegetables. Crumble goat cheese on top of roasted veggies, if desired. Bake the crostata for 20 to 25 minutes until the crust is golden and the eggs are set.

Can be served warm or at room temperature.

Onion Fennel Fritters

Fennel grows all over the Greek islands and the mainland, as it does here in the Ojai Valley. The spice is sometimes sold under the name "anise" because they share a similar taste profile—reminiscent of licorice—but fennel and anise are two different plants. While visiting Greece with my longtime BFF Kristina K., we devoured these fritters often with her family on the island of Zakynthos. Pan-fried in a little olive oil, these fritters are tender on the inside and pleasantly crunchy on the outside; I love the combination of caramelized onions and fennel which I also use on focaccia for a topping. Brown rice and garbanzo bean flours make this dish gluten free. MAKES ABOUT 12 FRITTERS

what you need

- 1 large onion, peeled, cut in ½ and thinly sliced
- 1 fennel bulb, cut in ½ and thinly sliced
- 1 garlic clove, minced
- 1 cup fresh chopped kale or other leafy greens, stems removed
- 3 large eggs
- ⅓ cup brown rice flour
- ⅓ cup garbanzo bean flour
- ¼ teaspoon baking soda
- ⅛ teaspoon cayenne pepper
- ½ teaspoon freshly ground pepper
- 1 teaspoon ground coriander
- 2 teaspoons of *A Taste of Ojai Wild Fennel Sea Salt* or your favorite sea salt
- 1 cup of olive oil for cooking

how to make it

In a medium bowl, add onion, fennel, garlic, and kale, and stir in 3 eggs.

Add rice and bean flours, baking soda, pepper, coriander, and salt; mix until just combined. (Avoid over mixing, which can make it starchy and gooey.)

Heat a skillet on medium heat for 2 minutes, then add olive oil to coat the bottom of the pan.

In batches, drop spoonfuls of the mixture into the hot oil without crowding. You want to hear the sizzle so make sure the pan has been preheated. Determine the size by whether you want mini bites for appetizers or a larger small-plate first course.

Fry about 2 to 3 minutes until each side has a golden brown crust.

With a slotted spatula, transfer fritters to a paper towel.

Sprinkle immediately with fennel sea salt and serve with Cucumber Tzatziki Sauce (see recipe on page 33).

....

Tip: You can make everything in advance. Just keep the fritters warm in the oven and the tzatziki sauce in the fridge.

Cucumber Tzatziki Sauce

Don't overthink this. It's a quick, cool sauce you can whip up in minutes with lots
of variations to suit many tastes.

what you need

1 cup nonfat plain Greek yogurt

½ cup cucumber, chopped small

1 garlic clove, peeled and minced

squirt of fresh lemon juice

pinch of chopped dill or fennel fronds

salt

freshly ground pepper

how to make it

Mix all the ingredients in a bowl and add a bit more
of this or that until the sauce meets your approval.
Feel free to add other favorite seasonings or herbs
such as fresh cilantro or ground coriander.

Charred Tomato Crostini

In Ojai, heirloom tomatoes just start to appear in late June and July at our farmers' market and CSA boxes. Oftentimes, because of our extended hot weather, we are lucky enough to have them all the way through October. Of course, flavors vary with combinations of different colors and varieties.

Often I pair heirloom tomatoes with *burrata*, a fresh mozzarella with a creamy center, or a local goat's milk Feta that's sold right here on Sunday mornings. With the addition of a handful of fresh herbs and a drizzle of syrupy aged balsamic atop crispy garlic-rubbed bread, it's the perfect summer appetizer or a quick savory breakfast. This recipe is more like assembling than cooking.

what you need

ripe cherry tomatoes (or large vine-ripened tomatoes, quartered)

extra-virgin olive oil

A Taste of Ojai Culinary Sea Salts or your favorite sea salt

freshly ground pepper

cheese (whatever's on hand: goat cheese, fresh mozzarella, blue, or your favorite)

fresh basil, thyme, parsley and/or mint

fresh baked rustic loaf of bread, sliced in thick ½-inch" slices

garlic cloves, peeled

aged balsamic vinegar

how to make it

Preheat broiler.

In a bowl, toss cherry or quartered tomatoes in a bit of olive oil and flavored sea salt and place them in a single layer on an oil-brushed baking sheet.

Place under the broiler for about 30 minutes until they are charred and blistered but not dried. You may need to rotate the pan and move the tomatoes around a bit to char all of them.

While tomatoes are charring, crumble or slice cheese and roughly chop the basil, thyme, parsley and/or mint.

Toast the bread and put in on a baking sheet. Rub each piece of toast with a peeled raw garlic clove, scraping it across the bread in one or two strokes.

Remove roasted tomatoes from oven and spoon onto the garlic-rubbed toast, then scatter with cheese, fresh herb's, sea salt, pepper, a bit more olive oil, and a drizzle of aged balsamic vinegar.

....

Tip: There are many flavored balsamic vinegars available now, so try a few and see which you like best. I love using fig balsamic, vanilla-infused balsamic, or, for a splash of heat, a dense chili-infused balsamic.

Frittata Toscana

Everyone has a delicious dish that's so deceptively simple they can make it by heart. I love frittatas because you can throw in whatever vegetables, herbs, and cheeses you happen to have in your fridge and it's a snap to pop it in the oven. This is one you'll want to commit to memory for a brunch or simple breakfast for dinner. MAKES 6 SERVINGS

what you need

6 large farm fresh eggs

½ teaspoon sea salt

freshly ground pepper

1 tablespoon olive oil, plus extra
   for brushing the pan

½ teaspoon fresh thyme, chopped

2 tablespoons fresh parsley leaves,
   chopped

FILLING SUGGESTIONS:

2 tablespoons olive oil

1 small zucchini, sliced thin

2 scallions, chopped

1 teaspoon garlic, minced

2 cups kale or other leafy greens, chopped

¼ cup soft sun-dried tomatoes,
   cut into strips

½ cup cooked potatoes or
   leftover rice or pasta

4 ounces mild cheese, cut into ¼-inch cubes
   grated cheddar, jack, feta or brie
   whatever's on hand

how to make it

Preheat the oven to 350°F.

In a medium bowl, crack eggs and gently whisk with salt, pepper, olive oil, thyme, and parsley.

Heat a 9-inch skillet (cast iron is best) on medium for a few minutes, then add 2 tablespoons of olive oil, zucchini, scallions, and garlic, and sauté for 4 or 5 minutes. You want to hear the sizzle when you add the vegetables to the pan. Continue sautéing until the vegetables start to caramelize. Add in kale or other greens and stir to wilt, then stir in sun-dried tomatoes and cooked potatoes to heat through.

Pour egg mixture directly into the skillet over the cooked vegetables and top with cheese.

Bake in the oven for 20 to 25 minutes, until puffed, golden, and set.

To make mini frittatas:

Brush a 12 cup muffin pan well with olive oil and place it on a baking sheet, so it's easier to put in and take out of oven. Spoon the cooked vegetable mixture into the holes, filling each halfway. Top with cheese, then spoon in the egg mixture.

Bake these minis for 15 to 20 minutes, until puffed, golden, and set.

Cool for 5 minutes, then gently run a round-bladed knife around the inside of each muffin cup. Carefully lift out or tap onto a serving platter. Serve warm with arugula salad tossed simply with olive oil and serve my Spicy Tomato Chili Jam alongside (see recipe on page 81).

Carmelized Fennel and Orange Salad

Fennel is an aromatic herb and surprisingly, a member of the carrot family and grows wild in the hills and mountains around Ojai. It has a large pale green bulb, celery-like stems and feathery leaves. Sliced thinly, the fennel bulb can be used in salads or served with other vegetables and a dip. Uncooked fennel has a mild licorice flavor and crunchy texture, while cooked fennel becomes more delicate and the texture softens. In this bright sophisticated salad, something magical happens on the palate when pairing fresh citrus with caramelized fennel and red onion, Use blood oranges when in season. Garnish with a cooling spoonful of yogurt or salty feta cheese. MAKES 2 SERVINGS

what you need

1 tablespoon extra-virgin olive oil

2 teaspoons ground coriander

2 tablespoons white sugar

1 navel orange (zest 1 tablespoon
    for garnish, then remove peel and pith
    and cut into ½-inch rounds)

2 tablespoons extra-virgin olive oil

1 fennel bulb, cut into ¼-inch-thin slices

½ red onion, cut into ¼-inch slices

1 teaspoon ground coriander

1 teaspoon of *A Taste of Ojai Wild Fennel
    Sea Salt* or your favorite sea salt

freshly ground pepper

¼ cup ouzo

2 tablespoons toasted walnuts,
    for garnish

how to make it

In a medium sauté pan just large enough to hold one layer of orange slices, heat 1 tablespoon olive oil on medium high heat.

Add coriander and sugar. When sugar has melted and started to caramelize, lower heat to medium and add the orange slices. Cook 1 or 2 minutes, turn slices over, cook for another minute, and remove pan from heat. Set orange slices aside on a dish. Pour hot water on the pan to rinse off the sugar, discard, wipe clean and return pan to the stove on medium heat.

Add 2 tablespoons of olive oil to cover the bottom of the pan. When it's hot, add the fennel and red onion slices, generously sprinkle with ground coriander, sea salt, and pepper, and sear for 5 minutes to caramelize.

Stir in ouzo, and cook for 2 more minutes.

Arrange the salad components on serving plates. Layer the orange slices on top, sprinkle lightly with *A Taste of Ojai Wild Fennel Sea Salt* and freshly ground pepper, drizzle with good local extra-virgin olive oil, and garnish with toasted walnuts and orange zest.

Serve with a dollop of nonfat Greek yogurt or a slice of feta cheese.

Gorgonzola Stuffed Figs

Late summer into the autumn months our fig trees are full of fresh ripe fruit, and I get to have fun preparing this effortless, full-of-flavor indulgence. When fresh figs are no longer abundant, I substitute dried figs or pitted dates—they're equally as good if not better. Use a soft triple-cream blue cheese or sweet gorgonzola, or cut the blue cheese with a bit of cream cheese for a milder filling. Served with a glass of sherry or local red wine, it's heaven. MAKES 24

what you need

24 fresh figs, dried figs, or pitted dates

4 ounces gorgonzola dolce blue cheese at room temperature (or your favorite creamy blue)

Sea salt and freshly ground pepper

½ cup Pomegranate Glaze (see recipe on page 87) or aged balsamic vinegar

24 walnut halves, toasted (you may substitute chopped toasted pecans or chopped toasted pistachios)

how to make it

Make a slit in the figs or dates but not all the way through.

Whip the blue cheese with a sturdy whisk or food processor and season generously with sea salt and pepper. Spoon some cheese into the slit of the fruit and pinch closed. Top each with a toasted walnut half or chopped toasted nuts. Drizzle with my Pomegranate Glaze or aged balsamic and serve on a tray for a flavorful bite with cocktails.

....

Tip: You'll have leftover gorgonzola filling, so spoon it into a bowl, cover, and refrigerate for later as a topping for other delights, spread on pizza for a topping.

Roasted Sweet Potatoes and Figs

As an appetizer or small-plate first course, this unusual combination uses fresh, ripe figs and sweet potatoes. The addition of my Pomegranate Glaze rounds up the flavors. SERVES 4

what you need

2 large sweet potatoes

5 tablespoons olive oil

2 teaspoons of *A Taste of Ojai Wild Fennel Sea Salt*

1 teaspoon freshly ground pepper

3 spring onions, halved lengthwise and cut into 2-inch-long segments

1 red chili, thinly sliced or ½ teaspoon red chili flakes

4 tablespoons Pomegranate Glaze (see recipe on page 87) or aged balsamic vinegar

8 fresh, ripe figs or dried mission figs, quartered

4 ounces soft goat cheese, crumbled (optional)

how to make it

Preheat oven to 425°F. Drizzle a baking sheet with 2 tablespoons of olive oil.

Scrub the sweet potato skins well, cut in half lengthwise, then cut each half lengthwise again into four long wedges. You will have a total of 16 wedges. In a bowl, toss them with 2 tablespoons olive oil, sea salt and pepper. On the baking sheet, lay out the wedges and roast for 25 to 30 minutes, flip the wedges over after about 15 minutes, until golden brown. Arrange the sweet potatoes on a serving plate.

Heat a medium-size sauté pan with 1 tablespoon of olive oil, add the spring onions and red chili, and fry on medium heat for 3 to 4 minutes, stirring often so the chili doesn't burn. Drizzle in about 2 tablespoons of Pomegranate Glaze and stir. Add the quartered figs and toss to heat through. Spoon this warm mixture over the roasted sweet potatoes, drizzle with a little more Pomegranate Glaze and top with crumbled goat cheese, if desired.

Serve warm.

Tomato Rissoles

From our Greek island visits with bestie Kristina K, this delicious Greek *mezze* or small dish originates from the island of Santorini. Making these brings back memories of our moped rides to watch the spectacular sunsets in Oia on the island's west side. The best part about making rissoles is squeezing the tomatoes to release the pulp.   MAKES 12-16

what you need

4 ripe tomatoes

3 ounces feta cheese

½ cup red onion, grated

1 tablespoon fresh parsley leaves, finely chopped

1 tablespoon fresh mint, finely chopped

1 teaspoon dried oregano

2 teaspoons of *A Taste of Ojai Pink Moment Sea Salt* or your favorite sea salt

freshly ground pepper

½ cup garbanzo bean flour

1 teaspoon baking powder

Olive oil for frying

3 tablespoons capers, drained and dried on a paper towel

how to make it

Put the tomatoes in a large bowl and squeeze them with your hands, so the pulp comes out and you are left with a chunky mixture. No need to remove the skins.

In a separate bowl, mash the feta cheese with a fork, then mix in the grated onion, parsley, mint oregano, sea salt, and pepper. Mix in the chunky tomato mixture, garbanzo flour and baking powder and stir to combine until it forms a thick, moist, sticky paste that is firm enough to form balls. Refrigerate the mixture for 30 minutes.

In a medium cast iron skillet or sauté pan over medium heat, add about ½ inch of olive oil to cover the bottom. Dip a tablespoon in water (so pasty mixture won't stick) and add spoonfuls of mixture into the hot oil. Repeat, dipping the spoon in water each time, making sure each spoonful of mixture doesn't touch another.

Fry the tomato rissoles for 2 to 3 minutes on each side, until golden brown.

Using a slotted spatula, transfer them to a paper towel to drain. Immediately sprinkle some *Pink Moment Sea Salt* on top of the cooked rissoles. Continue to make in batches with the rest of the batter.

Afterward, add the capers to the same hot oil and fry on medium heat until the little buds start to open and look crisp. Be careful not to burn them. With a slotted spoon, transfer them onto paper towels; they will continue to crisp as they cool.

Arrange the rissoles on a serving platter and top with the fried capers and extra feta cheese. Enjoy this Santorini island recipe with some crusty bread, yogurt, and, of course, a sip of ouzo. Opa!

Fried Haloumi with Pears and Spiced Dates

Many Mediterranean-themed parties start with *haloumi*, a sheep's milk cheese from Cyprus. However, you have to travel no farther than Whole Foods Market or Trader Joes to buy it. This mild, salty cheese is a great small-plate first course and can be served on toasted pieces of bread as an appetizer. I love the use of fragrant sweet spices with this cheese as well as ouzo, my favorite anise-flavored Greek liqueur. *Yiamas!* In other words: To your health. MAKES 4 SERVINGS

what you need

1 lemon

1 tablespoon dark brown sugar

¼ teaspoon ground cumin

¼ teaspoon ground coriander

⅛ teaspoon ground cardamom

⅛ teaspoon freshly ground pepper

8 dates, halved and pitted

2 tablespoons olive oil, divided

8 ounces haloumi cheese, cut into 8 slices ⅓ inch thick

1 unpeeled firm pear, quartered, seeded, and sliced lengthwise into 12 pieces

8 slices of a rustic country bread loaf

2 tablespoons ouzo

how to make it

Heat the oven to 350°F.

Zest and juice the lemon. In a small sauté pan on medium heat, cook brown sugar with lemon zest and juice, stirring until the sugar just starts to melt, about 2 minutes. Stir in the cumin, coriander, cardamom, black pepper, and dates, and cook until dates soften, about 3 to 4 minutes. Stir in 1 tablespoon of olive oil, remove pan from heat, and set aside.

Heat a large, nonstick pan over medium-high for 2 minutes, then arrange all the haloumi slices in the pan, without overlapping them. Brown the cheese, 1 to 2 minutes on each side. (You will not need to add oil while cooking the cheese. If the pan is warmed up first, then your haloumi will have a nice crust to it.)

Transfer the cheese to a heavy baking dish just large enough to hold the slices in a single layer without overlapping. In the same nonstick pan, heat 1 tablespoon olive oil over medium-high, and add the pear slices in a single layer. Brown the pears on each side, 1 to 2 minutes per side.

Transfer the pears to the baking dish and layer over the haloumi. Spoon the spiced date mixture over the pears and place the baking dish in the oven. Heat until the pears are warmed and the cheese is softened, about 5 minutes. Meanwhile, toast the bread and place it on a serving dish or platter.

Remove the baking dish to the countertop and pour ouzo over the top. Ignite the ouzo with a long match (do this carefully as the flames will spread quickly and can reach several inches high) and flambé the mixture. When the flames die out after about a minute or so, spoon the pears, dates, and cheese over the toast. Serve immediately.

Zucchini Kofta
in Spiced Tomato Sauce

In the simplest form, *koftas*, made in many Middle Eastern and Indian cultures, consist of ground meat—usually beef or lamb—mixed with spices and onions, and are often shaped into meatballs. The recipe for these vegetarian meatless "meatballs" are infused with fragrant warming spices, in a rich coconut-tomato sauce. I guarantee you won't miss the meat. MAKES 12 PIECES

what you need

FOR THE KOFTA

1 cup zucchini, grated

1 cup potatoes, peeled and boiled until tender, and drained

½ cup spring onions, finely chopped

3 tablespoons garbanzo bean flour

3 tablespoons brown rice flour

1 tablespoon garam masala

¼ teaspoon cumin

2 tablespoons fresh cilantro leaves, chopped

2 green chilies, chopped

1 teaspoon Sea Salt

½ teaspoon freshly ground pepper

pinch of cayenne pepper

vegetable oil for frying

what you need

FOR THE SAUCE

1 tablespoon coconut oil

1 cinnamon stick

¼ teaspoon turmeric

pinch cayenne, or more if desired

2 teaspoons ground coriander

1 teaspoon garam masala

1 tablespoon Ginger Garlic Paste (see recipe on page 88)

2 cups tomatoes, finely chopped (or canned organic diced tomatoes, drained)

1 teaspoon of *A Taste of Ojai Pink Moment Sea Salt* with Pink Peppercorns or your favorite sea salt

½ cup light coconut milk

1 teaspoon fresh lime juice

how to make the Kofta

In a large bowl, mix zucchini, cooked potatoes, and spring onions. Add the garbonzo bean and brown rice flours, garam masala, cumin, cilantro and green chilies. Season with salt and pepper.

Mix to combine.

In a medium skillet, heat about 1-inch of vegetable oil for 3 to 4 minutes on medium. With wet hands, gently form mixture into oblong balls. The mixture may feel a little loose and sticky, but once the balls hit the hot oil they will crisp up nicely. Fry in batches, turning each to achieve a light golden brown on all sides. Set aside and repeat until all are cooked.

how to make the sauce

In a medium saucepot, combine coconut oil, cinnamon stick, turmeric, cayenne, coriander, garam masala and sea salt. Stir over medium heat, Once they sizzle, stir in Ginger-Garlic Paste and chopped tomatoes.

Cook the tomatoes to reduce all the liquid, about 10 minutes. Remove the cinnamon stick and puree the sauce in a blender, with coconut milk. Return sauce to saucepot and simmer on low for 8 to 10 minutes until thick. To finish, add lime juice and mix well. (The sauce gets thicker as it sits,

so if you plan to serve it later, add a splash of water and heat it before serving.)

Pour the sauce into an ovenproof serving dish and arrange the koftas on top. Lightly shake the dish to coat the koftas. This can be kept warm in a 250°F oven for 30 minutes.

Serve as a small plate or as I do—with saffron rice and a simple salad. It's also great with flatbread.

Blistered Tomato Soup

Soup is quick and easy. I consider it my comfort food year round. When tomatoes are in abundance and the soup craving hits, i like to cook up this blistered version. It can be served in small quantities in shot glasses or paired perfectly with grilled cheese on a small plate. MAKES ONE QUART

what you need

2 pints tomatoes

Extra-virgin olive oil

1 teaspoon of *A Taste of Ojai Fennel Sea Salt* or your favorite sea salt

½ teaspoon freshly ground pepper

1 clove garlic, peeled and minced

1 medium onion, peeled and diced

2 carrots, peeled and diced

2 stalks celery, diced

1 teaspoon fresh ginger, peeled and minced

1 ½ cups canned chopped tomatoes like POMI brand or fire-roasted canned tomatoes

2 cups vegetable stock or water

½ cup vermouth or white wine

2 tablespoons balsamic vinegar

2 teaspoons fresh lemon juice

1 tablespoon Sriracha sauce or red chili flakes, optional

4 sprigs of fresh basil

how to make it

Preheat oven to 350°F.

In a bowl, toss fresh tomatoes with 2 tablespoons olive oil, salt, and pepper and put them on a parchment lined baking sheet, in a single layer. Roast in the oven for about 30 minutes, until tomatoes are blistered but not dried.

In a heavy-bottomed 2-quart pot over medium heat, add a few douses of olive oil and sauté the garlic, onion, carrot, celery, and ginger (or use 1 cup of Sofrito—see recipe on page 89—in place of the garlic and onions), until the vegetables are soft and fragrant, about 8 to10 minutes.

Add the oven-blistered tomatoes, the canned tomatoes, vegetable stock, and vermouth. Simmer for about 15 minutes. To finish, add the balsamic vinegar, 2 tablespoons extra-virgin olive oil, fresh lemon juice, and sriracha sauce. Using an immersion blender directly in the pot, or working in small batches in a blender, puree the soup until it is smooth. Season with additional salt and pepper, to taste. Top with fresh basil sprigs. We topped ours with mini grilled cheese bites.

Goat Cheese Truffles

When friends drop in unexpectedly, this is my go-to appetizer. These truffles are no-cook and finger-friendly. The addition of crushed pistachios and fresh herbs make them a savory sensation, but once you familiarize yourself with this recipe, the sky's the limit: Go wild adding different types of nuts, crushed seeds, your favorite herbs, and freshly ground spices. MAKES ABOUT 2 DOZEN

what you need

1 cup pistachios or other nuts, finely chopped

2 teaspoons thyme, finely chopped

2 teaspoons tarragon, finely chopped

2 teaspoons chives, finely chopped

8 ounces goat cheese

A Taste of Ojai Lavender Sea Salt or your favorite sea salt, to taste

freshly ground pepper

6 dried apricots or other dried fruit, quartered

¼ cup Balsamic jam (page 75)

how to make it

Put the nuts in one bowl and the chopped herbs and chives into another bowl, setting aside a small amount of herbs for the cheese mixture.

In another bowl, mix the goat cheese with salt, pepper, and 2 teaspoons of the reserved chopped herbs.

Using your hands, roll the cheese mixture into 1-inch balls. Using your thumb, make a hole in each ball, press an apricot piece into the center, and then mold the cheese around the apricot. (you can omit this step and just roll up the goat cheese without the dried fruit)

Roll some of the balls in the chopped pistachios and some in the chopped herbs. Then place all of them on a parchment-lined baking sheet and chill.

If you make these earlier take them out of the refrigerator 20 minutes before serving to serve at room temperature.

For an impressive presentation, drizzle or "paint" a serving tray with balsamic jam and set the truffles on top or add these goat cheese truffles to a simple salad of fresh market greens for a small plate.

You can make these up to two days before serving and store in the refrigerator.

....

Tip: Be imaginative and roll these little morsels in herbs and spices with different textures and colors, such as chopped parsley and thyme, chopped almonds, crushed cumin seeds, or even matcha green tea powder, turmeric or smoked paprika.

Socca

My first time eating socca, also known as farinata or torta di ceci, was on a trip I took to Italy 25 years ago with good friend, fellow chef, and award-winning cookbook author Pamela Sheldon-Johns. We took a side trip to the southern coast of France and spent a food-filled fantasy weekend in Nice before heading back to Tuscany. I remember watching a street vendor meticulously creating crepe batter and cooking it in a huge pan on a stove. The result was this peppery chickpea crepe. We picked it up with our fingers and devoured it piping hot.

Often for breakfast I make a sweet version, omitting the pepper and simply drizzling it with organic honey. Sometimes I throw sliced toasted almonds and fresh berries on top. This simple batter is nothing more than chickpea flour, water, and olive oil and happens to be gluten free. MAKES TWO 9-INCH CRÊPES

what you need

1 cup garbanzo bean flour sifted

1¼ cups water

1 tablespoon olive oil, plus more for cooking

½ teaspoon sea salt

½ teaspoon freshly ground pepper

Socca is done, when top is browned and dough pulls slightly away from the edges.

how to make it

Preheat oven to 400°F and place a small cast-iron skillet in the oven for 10 minutes. Using oven mitts, remove the skillet and coat with a generous amount of olive oil; this will be soaked up into the crepe.

Position the oven rack on the upper level. Pour about half of the batter in the skillet, place on the rack, and bake for about 10 minutes. You will see edges start to get crispy; batter should be firm in the center, not runny. The top will be slightly browned. Flip the socca out of the pan onto a serving plate.

For the second crepe, add more olive oil to the hot pan and pour the remaining batter into the skillet. If you prefer a slightly crispier crepe, place the finished crepes on a baking sheet and return to the oven for a few minutes.

....

Tip: Simply spread with some hummus and fresh herbs. Shown here with hummus, grilled onions and fresh chopped cilantro.

Cast-Iron Skillet Tips

If you haven't cooked with cast iron before, it's a great option but takes getting used to. Cooking with it has healthful benefits, it fortifies your food with iron & it's a chemical-free alternative to nonstick pans. When properly seasoned a cast-iron pan will last years & does not require much oil or butter. **Here are some cleaning tips:**

- Avoid soaking the pan or using the dishwasher, do not leave it in the sink, it will rust.

- Wash the skillet by hand using hot water a sponge or stiff brush & to remove stuck-on food, scrub the pan with a paste of coarse salt & water. Avoid soap or steel wool, as these can strip the pan's seasoning.

- Thoroughly towel dry or dry on the stove over low heat.

- Once dry, use a cloth or paper towel to apply a light coat of olive oil to the inside of the skillet so it doesn't rust.

- Some cooks also like to oil the outside of the skillet. Buff to remove any excess and store in a dry place.

Spanish Gazpacho

Gazpacho provides a cool and refreshing start to a meal on a hot summer day. Since I've lived in Malaga, Spain, which is part of Andalusia, where gazpacho originates—I can vouch for this recipe's authenticity as I observed it being made many times on scorching hot days. I've added a touch of smokiness with Spanish smoked **pimentón.** And as in Spain, only homegrown tomatoes or those from the farmers' markets are used, often using those that have gotten overripe from the sun. It's best to make this in the morning so it's well chilled, to serve later in the afternoon. MAKES ONE QUART

what you need

4 slices country bread, broken into big chunks, crusts removed

2 pounds very ripe tomatoes, coarsely chopped

1 cucumber, peeled, and cut into small dice

1 red bell pepper, seeds and pith removed, chopped rough

2 garlic cloves, peeled and smashed

½ cup extra-virgin olive oil

1 teaspoon of your favorite sea salt

½ teaspoon Spanish pimentón (smoked paprika)

2 tablespoons viniagre de Jerez (Spanish sherry vinegar)

½ cup water or tomato juice, as needed

½ white onion, diced small for garnish

how to make it

Put bread chunks in a medium bowl with tomatoes, ¾ of the cucumber, red pepper, garlic, ¼ cup olive oil, and salt. Mix to combine and let sit for 20 to 30 minutes so flavors marry and salt pulls some moisture out of the tomatoes.

Puree the tomato-bread mixture in a high speed blender with the pimentón, sherry vinegar, and remaining olive oil. It should have a "drinkable" consistency, as generally it is served in small glasses. Blend in a little cold water or tomato juice to loosen the mixture, if needed. Taste and add more salt as needed. Transfer to a large pitcher or bowl. Chill for at least 2 hours.

Garnish with the remaining chopped cucumber, chopped onion, and a small cruet of vinegar and serve cold.

....

Tip: My preference is omitting the onion from the gazpacho recipe and serving it as an optional garnish on the side. To impress, serve in small shot glasses and hang a chilled cocktail shrimp off each glass or add a spoonful of fresh crabmeat on top. If you desire a gluten-free version, leave out the bread.

Condiments,
Spreads & Sauces

Concetta's Bruschetta Sun-Dried Tomato Spread

I first prepared this yummy spread for actress Connie Sellecca and her husband, radio and TV host John Tesh, on the eve of their wedding rehearsal. That was 20-plus years ago, and ever since, it has become a favorite start to their family Christmas dinner every year. The bruschetta—which I renamed in Connie's honor—complements the authentic Italian dishes I prepare for their special holiday celebration. SERVES 6

what you need

7 ounce jar of sun-dried tomatoes, packed in oil

2 teaspoons capers, drained

2 teaspoons pitted Kalamata olives

2 garlic cloves, peeled

8 fresh basil leaves

½ cup feta cheese

2 tablespoon extra-virgin olive oil

1 tablespoon balsamic vinegar

salt

freshly ground pepper

2 baguettes

how to make it

Drain the sun-dried tomatoes, reserving the oil.

In the bowl of a food processor, put in the sun-dried tomatoes, capers, pitted olives, and garlic.

Pulse the processor to break down the mixture, and then add the basil, Feta, 1 tablespoon of reserved tomato oil, olive oil, and balsamic vinegar, with a few grinds of freshly ground pepper. The capers, olives and feta are salty, so taste it first before adding salt.

To serve, scoop the spread into a bowl and arrange a plate with toasted baguette slices. Grab a slice and spoon on a generous amount of Concetta's bruschetta spread. **Buono!**

Fig and Olive Tapenade

An impressive combination of figs and olives giving this tapenade a unique twist.

MAKES 2 CUPS

what you need

½ cup dried black mission figs, chopped

2 tablespoon olive oil

2 tablespoons balsamic vinegar

1 teaspoon dried thyme

⅛ teaspoon red chili flakes

1 cup pitted Kalamata olives

2 fresh garlic cloves, peeled

½ cup shelled pistachios, toasted

3 ounces feta cheese, crumbled

½ teaspoon *A Taste of Ojai Lavender Sea Salt* or your favorite sea salt

¼ teaspoon freshly ground pepper

how to make it

In a food processor, combine figs, olive oil, balsamic vinegar, thyme, and red chili. Pulse to break down the mixture, then add pitted olives, garlic, and pistachios, and pulse again until mixed but not pureed. Stir in crumbled feta cheese, and season with *A Taste of Ojai Lavender Sea Salt* and pepper. Transfer to a glass container, cover and refrigerate for 4 hours or overnight to allow flavors to meld.

Serve as a great dip with slices of bread or my homemade Lavender-Fig Crackers (see recipe on page 98). It's also a wonderful accompaniment to grilled lamb.

Roasted Vegetable Hummus

Oh gosh, you're thinking, "Not another hummus recipe." I love hummus. It's the most delicious and quick answer to "What do I have to eat in the fridge?" Plus, it's a great way of using all those gorgeous vegetables you get weekly in the Community Support Box. Just clean and cut all those beautiful crunchy raw vegetables and arrange them on a pretty platter with this easy-to-make hummus. I like to serve it warm.

MAKES ABOUT 3 CUPS

what you need

3 pounds of vegetables for roasting (such as turnips, rutabagas, parsnips, carrots, celery root, sweet potatoes, or winter squash), scrubbed and cut into 1-inch pieces

2 tablespoons extra-virgin olive oil

1 large shallot, peeled and sliced

2 cloves garlic, peeled and smashed

1 teaspoon sea salt

1 teaspoon freshly ground pepper

2 lemons, juiced

¼ cup tahini sesame paste

2 tablespoons extra-virgin olive oil

2 teaspoons of *A Taste of Ojai Pink Moment Sea Salt*

how to make it

Preheat oven to 350°F. In a bowl, toss vegetables together in olive oil with shallot and garlic. Season well with salt and pepper and put on 2 lightly oiled baking sheets to roast.

When you put the vegetables in the oven, raise the heat to 400°F and roast for 35 to 40 minutes. Flip the vegetables over once during roasting until roots are caramelized and tender. Remove from oven and cool slightly before you make the dip.

Making in 2 batches, Place half of the roasted vegetables in a food processor and add the juice of 1 lemon, ½ of the tahini paste, 1 tablespoon extra-virgin olive oil, 1 teaspoon sea salt, and a few tablespoons of water, and blend until pureed . Pour mixture into a bowl and set aside. Again, in the food processor, puree the rest of the vegetables, lemon juice, tahini paste, olive oil, sea salt, and water. Pour into the bowl with the first batch and combine.Arrange a platter of fresh, cut raw vegetables. You can serve the hummus warm or slightly chilled, whatever you prefer. The hummus will hold for three days in the fridge—if you don't eat it all the first day.

Tip: Choose a single hue of vegetable for the dip. Substitute veggies such as carrots with sun-dried tomato or roasted pepper, sweet potatoes, or buttered squash for a dazzling orange dip or beets for a vivid magenta. When using beets, make sure to roast them on a separate tray and blend them separately in the food processor. Be creative with your own version.

Kale Pesto

Kale adds a rich earthy note and brilliant green color to this hearty dairy-free pesto made with both omega-rich hemp seeds and flaxseed oil. Best of all, it can be made in less than 5 minutes. Experiment with olive oil, walnut oil, or pistachio oil in place of the flaxseed oil. Nuts can be raw or toasted; any variation adds an element of flavor. Use as a dip with bread, rolled into grilled zucchini strips for a small bite, a marinade for grilled shrimp, a sandwich spread, in scrambled eggs, or in soup. Can you tell I love this pesto? The possibilities are endless. MAKES ABOUT 2 CUPS

what you need

2 garlic cloves, peeled and smashed

3 cups (about 1 bunch) organic kale

5 sprigs fresh basil

½ cup hemp seeds

½ cup pistachio nuts, toasted

1 tablespoon lemon zest

2 tablespoons fresh lemon juice

½ teaspoon of *A Taste of Ojai Fennel Sea Salt* or your favorite sea salt and ground fennel

¼ teaspoon freshly ground pepper

¼ cup flaxseed oil or extra-virgin olive oil

optional:

⅓ cup parmesan, feta, or pecorino cheese, grated

pinch of red pepper flakes

how to make it

In a food processor, add the garlic cloves, kale, basil, hemp seeds, pistachio nuts, lemon zest and juice, salt, and pepper. Turn on the processor and drizzle in the oil. Process to blend, stopping to scrape down the sides of the processor as necessary. Add more lemon, salt, or pepper, to taste. To achieve a thinner consistency, add more oil, And if you're serving with pasta, you can add to pasta with some of the reserved pasta cooking water just before serving.

Red Pepper and Walnut Spread

Based on the Middle Eastern spread called muhammara, this sweet and piquant dip will exceed all expectations. It's acceptable to use jarred roasted peppers, but roasting your own adds a light smokiness that the jarred variety just doesn't have. This is super-simple to make and is bursting with flavor.   MAKES ABOUT 2 CUPS

what you need

2 red bell peppers

1 slice day-old bread or ½ cup breadcrumbs, which can be gluten free

1 cup organic walnuts

2 tablespoons pomegranate molasses or glaze (see Pomegrante Glaze recipe on page 87)

2 tablespoons honey

1 tablespoon balsamic vinegar

2 teaspoons cumin

2 teaspoons coriander

2 teaspoons smoked paprika

1 teaspoon red chili flakes

1 teaspoon of *A Taste of Ojai Fennel Sea Salt* or your favorite sea salt

¼ cup extra-virgin olive oil

how to make it

The easiest method for roasting peppers is on the stovetop. Turn a burner to the highest setting and set the peppers directly on the flame. Using a pair of tongs, turn the peppers until the skin is completely blackened. (You can also char peppers under the broiler or on a gas grill. Leave peppers whole and turn them every few minutes until the skin is blackened.)

Put the peppers in a paper bag, and close. The skin will loosen as the pepper steams, and once it's cooled down, you can easily remove the skin with your fingers. I find it helpful to do this under running water to rinse off the charred skin and seeds.

Put the clean roasted peppers in a food processor, followed by the rest of the ingredients.

Pulse the processor to chop and blend the mix, allowing the nuts to break down so the spread will have texture. Continue pulsing until all the elements are blended but still a bit chunky. Serve with breads, crackers, or fresh sliced cucumber.

Labne

Labne is a delicious creamy Middle Eastern cheese that is made from strained yogurt. It's simple to make, and you'll find it comes in handy for all sorts of cooking endeavors. Use it in baking, with a dessert, or on a cheese platter as a spread doused with a splash of good olive oil and Mediterranean spice mix.

what you need

16 ounces plain Greek yogurt

....

Tip. You can substitute the whey for other liquids when baking—it gives breads and pancakes a nice sourdough taste. The whey can also be added to protein shakes and use when fermenting vegetables. My favorite use is keeping Feta cheese fresh by submerging it in whey as they often do in Greek delis.

how to make it

Line a colander with clean cheesecloth or a double layer of paper towels.

Scoop the yogurt onto the cloth and fold the cloth over the top of the yogurt to cover.

Place the colander in a large bowl to catch the whey with a small saucer underneath so the bottom of the colander is slightly lifted and not sitting in the liquid. Allow it to drain in the refrigerator overnight. The next day, transfer to a lidded glass container and refrigerate for up to 2 weeks. Save the liquid whey in a separate glass container.

Now that you have this simple base, here's just a few things you can do with labne:

• Top with roasted garlic, roasted bell peppers, and walnuts, douse it with a good fruity extra-virgin olive oil, and serve with crusty bread or lavosh crackers.

• Mix in ground cardamom, cinnamon, and a touch of rosewater and serve on the side of a cake or tart.

• Drizzle with local honey and a splash of orange juice and serve with toast.

• Roll into small balls, put them on a serving plate, and sprinkle with Middle Eastern za'atar spice mix and extra virgin olive oil.

Preserved Lemons

After getting a basketful of beautiful Meyer lemons from friends at Ocean Ranch Organics, I couldn't wait to make preserved lemons. This recipe combines both salt and sugar, making these preserves versatile in many dishes, both sweet and savory. A special preserving process requires making a brine, which is not unlike pickling and takes a bit of time. After ingredients are combined, they are left to loosen up to transform. Once you've preserved lemons, it's the rind, not the juice or pulp, that you'll be using in most recipes. After a few weeks you will have something that adds brilliance to a rice or grain dish, dressings, Moroccan tagines, or even in a Bloody Mary. The sweetness of the lemons is also a nice addition to yogurt-based sauces.

what you need

6 organic lemons

½ cup sugar

½ cup kosher salt

1 teaspoon crushed coriander seeds

¼ teaspoon turmeric

3 cloves

....

Tip: I add a preserved lemon when making homemade hummus in place of lemon juice. It adds an unusual mellow yet intensely lemony flavor, plus I end up using less salt.

how to make it

Set a large pot of water on the stove and bring to a boil.

Scrub lemons well and place into boiling water for 10 minutes.

With a slotted spoon, transfer lemons to an ice bath (a medium bowl filled with half ice and half cold water). Reserve 2 cups of the cooking liquid.

Mix sugar, salt, coriander seeds, turmeric, and cloves in a small bowl.

Score the lemons by cutting each into quarters but not all the way through to the other end. In a large bowl add the lemons with the sugar, salt, and spices from the small bowl. Then place the lemons in a clean 1-quart Mason jar. Sprinkle with any remaining sugar-salt-spice mixture, then pour reserved cooking liquid in and cover completely; you may have to push the lemons down with a wooden spoon to totally immerse them in the liquid. Cover with a lid and chill for 2 weeks in the refrigerator.

Once the lemons are preserved, many recipes call for using only the rind and discarding the membrane. I often use the whole lemon. When you remove a lemon from the brining liquid, push the seeds out with your fingers. Chop or puree the whole preserved lemon and add to your preparation.

Balsamic Black Pepper Jam

Don't be intimidated by making jam. I had a big bowl of strawberries left over from a brunch and made this batch in less than 10 minutes. It's simply fruit cooked down with sugar, lemon juice, and vinegar. And instead of filling a dozen jars for your pantry, just make a cup or two at a time, enough to last through the next week. I like this peppery jam for savory dishes, and it's exceptional on morning toast. MAKES ABOUT 1 PINT

what you need

4 cups strawberries, washed and
  hulled (or raspberries, blackberries,
  or fresh figs)

½ cup sugar or sugar substitute

juice of half a lemon (about 1 tablespoon)

½ cup aged (or reduced) balsamic vinegar

1 teaspoon freshly ground pepper

pinch of sea salt

how to make it

In a bowl, stir together sliced berries sprinkled with sugar and allow to sit for about an hour before making the jam.

In a large skillet (cast iron is perfect) over medium-high heat, add berry-sugar mixture with juices, and lemon juice, stir often and break up any large chunks of berry with a wooden spoon, cook about 10 minutes. Add balsamic vinegar, pepper, and a generous pinch of salt, and stir to combine. Simmer an additional 5 minutes to thicken. Pour into a clean glass pint jar, cover and cool. Refrigerate and use within 3 weeks.

....

Tip: After the jam is made, you can puree it in a small blender, thinning out with a tablespoon of warm water, to use as a glaze for goat cheese truffles.

Orange-Fennel Mostarda

My introduction to this classic relish-like marmalade—Mostarda—came while I was exploring the small markets in Italy's northern regions in search of something special to eat with our standard midday meal of bread and cheese. Mostarda is an Italian condiment that's usually made of candied fruit and mustard-flavored syrup. Served with roasts at holiday dinners, it's a vibrant and welcome alternative to cranberry sauce.

This recipe is for a small batch, but you might want to make use of winter's fresh oranges while they are in season and make a large batch to store in jars for enjoyment all year long. And you don't have to use only oranges. Use a combination of citrus fruits to create your own version and serve with a platter of hard aged cheeses and cured meats. Or eat it straight out of the jar. MAKES ABOUT 1 PINT

what you need

1 small fennel bulb, cut into small dice

1 teaspoon whole mustard seeds

½ teaspoon whole fennel seeds

¼ cup brown sugar

¼ cup apple cider vinegar

6 tablespoons water

2 oranges (or combo of citrus fruits such as tangerines, clementines, blood oranges)

pinch of salt

how to make it

In a small saucepot, add fennel, mustard seeds, fennel seeds, sugar, vinegar, and water, then place on stove over medium heat.

Meanwhile, cut the two oranges into small dice with rind attached, removing any seeds. Add to the saucepot, which should be at a rapid simmer by now.

Raise heat so mixture boils for about 4 to 5 minutes, stirring occasiionally, then lower heat to medium. Simmer for another 10 minutes or until liquid is reduced to the consistency of maple syrup (nearly all liquid will be gone by then) and the mustard seeds have plumped and softened. Set aside and cool, then stir in a pinch of salt

At this point, the mostarda will still be chunky. If you want a more jam-like consistency, blend with a stick blender or in a mini blender. Refrigerate the mostarda in a small lidded jar.

If making a larger batch, store and label in glass jars, following proper canning procedures.

....

Tip: Homemade mostarda is great as a gift with a hunk of aged cheese, a small cutting board, and a cheese knife or an antique spoon.

Salsa Verde

It's been said that to make an authentic and flavorful salsa verde, fresh herbs must be chopped by hand. So I did, painstaking pulling every leaf from its stem and chopping. This is not the pale green salsa found on tamales. I just take everything and whiz it into my food processor for a fresh herbaceous sauce to serve as a dip.

Jazz up eggs, serve as an accompaniment to grilled fish and roasted meats, or brighten up soup with a few spoonfuls added before serving. This has become a staple on our condiment table.   MAKES 2 CUPS

what you need

2 garlic cloves, peeled

2 tablespoon capers

4 gherkins or small cornichons (or a pickle)

1 bunch flat-leaf parsley, leaves picked

6 sprigs fresh basil, leaves picked

1 handful fresh mint, leaves picked

1 tablespoon Dijon mustard

3 tablespoons fresh lemon juice

½ cup extra-virgin olive oil

A Taste of Ojai Wild Fennel Sea Salt or your favorite sea salt and freshly ground pepper to taste

how to make it

Put the garlic, capers, gherkins, and herbs into a food processor. Add Dijon mustard and lemon juice, and pulse the mixture while slowly drizzling in olive oil until all is blended and it is the consistency of pesto. Balance the flavors with a bit of salt and freshly ground pepper. The fresh lemon juice prevents the mixture from discoloring.

Covered in a glass jar and refrigerated, the salsa will last a good week.

Spicy Tomato Chili Jam

Tomato jam is like grown-up ketchup, and this bold fiery version is a cross between ketchup and sweet chili sauce. The warm, spicy flavor of ginger, gives this an Asian twist. The natural pectin in tomatoes provides a jammy consistency. As an essential condiment in our kitchen, it's used often on eggs and toast, as a glaze on fish and fowl, and as a spread with goat cheese to be served alongside a cheese board. MAKES 1 PINT

what you need

1 pound very ripe tomatoes, divided

2 red chilies or a pinch of red chili flakes

4 tablespoons Ginger-Garlic Paste (see recipe on page 88) or

4 peeled garlic cloves and a 2-inch piece of ginger, peeled and roughly chopped

3 tablespoons tamari

½ cup brown sugar

⅓ cup red wine vinegar

1 tablespoon balsamic vinegar

how to make it

In a food processor, puree half of the tomatoes with the chilies, Garlic-Ginger Paste, and tamari. In a medium pot on high heat, pour in tomato mixture along with brown sugar and red wine vinegar and slowly bring to a boil, stirring occasionally. When it reaches a boil, lower heat and simmer gently for 10 minutes.

Dice and add in the remaining tomatoes and add balsamic vinegar. Gently simmer for another 10 minutes, stirring every 3 minutes to release solids that settle on the bottom. Scrape the sides of the pot during cooking so mixture cooks evenly.

When it's cooked down, pour the warm jam into a clean glass jar with lid and allow to cool to room temperature. Store in refrigerator for up to 2 weeks.

Tip: As with relishes, chutneys, and other jams, this can be stored without refrigerating if you are familiar with preserving and canning procedures.

Lavender Mascarpone Spread

During the month of June it's all about lavender in Ojai. The fragrant, flowering shrub is in full bloom and casts a lovely bluish purple tint over the entire area. There's even a Lavender Festival here in Ojai that takes place to honor this earthy plant. As a component in this ultra-creamy Italian cheese spread, lavender adds subtle aroma and flavor. On desserts I often substitute this for whipped cream because of its luscious and creamy texture, add it to your cheese platter, or just savor it yourself in the morning atop an onion bagel, the Pear Tartine (page 22), or raisin toast.

what you need

¼ cup cream cheese, softened

¼ cup plain Greek yogurt

8 ounces mascarpone

2 teaspoons organic culinary lavender buds

1 teaspoon of *A Taste of Ojai Lavender Sea Salt* or your favorite sea salt

½ teaspoon freshly ground pepper

1 teaspoon fresh lemon zest

4 tablespoons local honey

1 tablespoon rosewater

how to make it

In a small bowl or food processor, blend all ingredients.

Lavender's aroma and flavor are instantly recognizable, which makes it a perfect unexpected culinary herb. Typically paired with dairy, such as custard or ice cream, it isn't just for desserts. Fittingly, lavender can bring an incredible spring feeling to a dish. Whisk it into vinaigrettes, toss it with roasted vegetables, or use when making risotto or rice. You can also use lavender in a marinade for grilled lamb. Dried lavender is a frequent addition to the herb blend Herbes de Provence which includes marjoram, rosemary, thyme, and fennel. Dried lavender can be used whole, but if you're making something with a silky-smooth texture, you may want to briefly run it through a spice grinder. Just make sure your lavender is clearly labeled food grade and is chemical and pesticide-free.

Tip: Rosewater accents lavender's floral note, adding a distinct Middle Eastern flavor. A little lemon zest gives it zip.

Root Vegetable Paté

You can roast any root vegetables to make this healthful indulgent vegan pâte with a Middle Eastern flavor. Serve with sliced warm bread or my aromatic Lavender Fig Crackers (see recipe on page 98). MAKES 2 CUPS

what you need

1 fennel bulb, roughly chopped

1 medium onion, sliced

2 cups of any combination of root vegetables: carrots, parsnips, sweet potatoes, celery root, or turnips, peeled and sliced

1 tablespoon grainy mustard

2 tablespoons extra-virgin olive oil

1 teaspoon ground toasted cumin

1 teaspoon ground toasted coriander

salt and freshly ground pepper to taste

1 teaspoon Pomegranate Glaze (see recipe on page 87) or balsamic vinegar

how to make it

Preheat oven to 400°F and line a baking sheet with parchment.

In a bowl, toss the fennel, onion, and root vegetables with grainy mustard, 1 tablespoon of olive oil, cumin, coriander, salt, and pepper. Using your hands, toss all until the vegetables are evenly coated, then transfer them to the baking sheet.

Roast the vegetables for about 30 minutes until fennel and onion have somewhat caramelized and the roots look shriveled and brown on the edges. Remove vegetables from oven and cool slightly.

Place vegetables in a food processor, adding the pomegranate glaze or balsamic vinegar. Pulse a few times to chop the vegetables, then add the remaining tablespoon of olive oil, continuing to puree, until you have a creamy pâte. If you desire a creamier consistency, add a tablespoon or two of water.

Spoon the mixture into a pretty bowl or line a mold with plastic wrap and spoon in the pâte and chill for an hour. Unmold to a plate and serve with pickles, toasted bread, roasted walnuts, or your favorite accompaniment.

....

Tip: For a different twist, switch out the root veggies with 1 pound of seasonal wild mushrooms, remove stems, slice, and roast with onion, fennel, and fresh thyme leaves for an earthy autumn spread.

Pomegranate Glaze

Sweet-tart pomegranate molasses combined with citrus juice contribute to this ruby glaze, a welcome element in many dishes. The star ingredient, pomegranate concentrate, is available in the beverage section of Middle Eastern, Asian, and Latin markets, as well as select gourmet supermarkets. Drizzle it on vegetables or fatty meats like leg of lamb and rib-eye steaks, as it adds a tantalizingly tart component. MAKES ABOUT 1 CUP

what you need

⅓ cup fresh juice from
    2 or 3 large oranges (or seasonal
    blood orange or tangerines)

¼ cup pomegranate concentrate

6 tablespoons honey

1 tablespoon balsamic vinegar

pinch of sea salt

how to make it

Strain fresh squeezed juice in a small saucepan, add pomegranate concentrate, honey, balsamic vinegar and sea salt. Simmer over medium-low heat until thick enough to coat the back of a spoon, about 10 minutes. Cool slightly before pouring into a lidded glass jar and store at room temperature.

Tip: This glaze is used in several of my recipes in this book, drizzled over my Figs stuffed with whipped gorgonzola, and has proven to work well with my roasted sweet potatoes with figs, goat cheese truffles, and in my roasted root vegetable pate.

Ginger Garlic Paste

Pungent ginger and garlic make a great marinade rub for beef, chicken and fish. Ginger acts as a tenderizer to make meats succulent, and I also often add this to broths and soups as a flavor enhancer. You will find many other uses for this versatile staple. Keep in mind it has salt, so let your taste buds dictate how much to use when you're seasoning your dish.

what you need

½ cup fresh garlic cloves, peeled

½ cup fresh ginger, peeled

1 teaspoon sea salt

3 tablespoons extra-virgin olive oil

how to make it

In a food processor, pulse all ingredients until a paste forms. Refrigerate in a lidded glass jar and use in your weekly preparations.

• For a hot version, toss a stemless green chile into the food processor with the garlic and ginger.

....

Tip: Spoon the mixture into ice cube trays, freeze, and pop out as needed.

Use in Spicy Tomato Sauce with Zucchini Kofta (see recipe on page 48) and Spicy Tomato Chili Jam (see recipe on page 81).

Sofrito

When I was a young cook in the kitchen my grandmother told me that the key to a good soup or sauce is the way that the onion is cooked—softly, gently, sweating in butter or olive oil. I have followed her advice ever since. The gently cooked onion is a foundation for flavor. It's magic. Instead of chopping garlic and onions every time you cook, use a ready-made version originating in Spain called sofrito. In France it's known as mirepoix or in Italy it's called soffritto. I want to share this basic recipe, because you'll see it as an ingredient in other recipes—use it to start off soups or add flavor to rice or risotto. If you make one big batch, it will save you tons of time and effort while adding extraordinary flavor to ordinary recipes.

what you need

1 head of garlic, peeled

2 large onions, peeled and sliced

2 large carrots, peeled and cut into large pieces

1 red chili (optional)

1 cup olive oil

how to make it

Place ingredients in a food processor and chop until coarse, pulsing the mixture but do not puree. Refrigerated in a lidded glass container, sofrito can be stored for a week. But you can always freeze in ice-cube trays for future use.

....

Tip: When cooking with sofrito, start off by slowly sautéing in butter or olive oil on medium low heat, before adding other ingredients.

Add a burst of flavor when using sofrito in Cauliflower Fritti (see recipe on page 28) and Blistered Tomato Soup (see recipe on page 51).

Crackers & Breads

Focaccia with Fennel and Caramelized onions

Focaccia dough is my go-to for pizza and almost any flatbread recipe. Caramelizing mellows fennels indicative licorice flavor. MAKES 1 FOCCACIA

what you need

FOR THE DOUGH:

1 cup warm water

1 tablespoon active dry yeast

3 cups all-purpose flour

3 tablespoons extra-virgin olive oil, plus extra for baking

1 teaspoon fresh rosemary, chopped fine

2 teaspoons of *A Taste of Ojai Fennel Sea Salt* or your favorite salt

FOR THE TOPPING:

2 tablespoons extra-virgin olive oil, plus extra for brushing

2 medium onions, halved lengthwise and thinly sliced

2 cups fennel, sliced

1 teaspoon of *A Taste of Ojai Wild Fennel Sea Salt* or your favorite course salt

1 teaspoon freshly ground pepper

1 cup Balsamic-Black Pepper Jam (see page 75)

6 ounces goat cheese crumbled, optional

how to make it

In a large bowl, in 1 cup of warm water, sprinkle yeast over the water, and stir well. When small bubbles start to form on the surface after 5 minutes or so, add 1½ cups of flour and stir well. Cover and let rest in a warm spot for 10 minutes.

Add another 1½ cups of flour, olive oil, chopped rosemary, and salt, and stir until a big mass of dough forms. On a well-floured work surface, turn out the dough and sprinkle it with 1 tablespoon of flour. Allow dough to rest and absorb flour for about 10 minutes.

Oil a clean bowl and set aside. Using a spatula or bench scraper, gently lift, fold, and press down the dough, then give it a quarter turn. Continue kneading and turning gently until the dough is smooth and elastic, about 12 turns, adding as little flour as possible. Place dough in the oiled bowl and turn it to coat, then cover with a tea towel and let rise for 1 hour.

WHILE THE DOUGH RISES, PREPARE THE TOPPING: In a large sauté pan on medium, heat 2 tablespoons of olive oil. Add sliced onions and fennel, liberally season with salt and pepper, and cook slowly until well browned and caramelized, 15 to 20 minutes. Remove from heat and set aside to cool.

Preheat oven to 450° F. Line a baking sheet with parchment paper and generously brush it with olive oil. Place dough on the oiled parchment and press it out with oiled hands into a 14 x 10-inch rectangle. It does not need to be perfectly shaped. Dimple the dough all over with your fingertips. Let it rest for 20 minutes.

Lightly drizzle it with more olive oil. Using an offset spatula or the back of a spoon, spread balsamic jam over the dough to within ½ inch of the edges. Cover jam with caramelized onions and fennel. Crumble goat cheese over the onions, if desired. Sprinkle with more salt and freshly ground pepper.

Bake dough until it is golden brown and cheese is bubbly and toasty, about 25 to 30 minutes. Cut into pieces and serve warm or at room temperature.

Rustic Cheese Galletas

Impress your guests with these super-easy and delicious rustic homemade crackers.

MAKES ABOUT 24 CRACKERS

what you need

½ stick unsalted butter, chilled and cubed, plus extra for pan

1 large egg, lightly beaten

1 cup all-purpose flour, plus extra for rolling

generous pinch each of sea salt and freshly ground pepper

½ cup parmesan or aged gouda cheese, grated

how to make it

Preheat oven to 350°F. Rub the surface of a baking sheet with butter .

Crack egg into a small bowl and beat with a fork. Set aside.

Sift the flour into a medium bowl and add salt and pepper. Mix the chilled butter into the flour. Using your fingertips, rub in the butter until the mixture resembles breadcrumbs. Stir in the cheese and half of the egg into the mixture to form the dough. Using your hands, work it into a ball.

Sprinkle flour on a work surface and turn the ball of dough onto it. With your hands, slightly flatten the ball. Sprinkle flour on rolling pin and on top of the dough, then roll dough to about a ¼ inch thin rectangle.

Using a pizza cutter or knife, cut dough into long ½-inch-thin strips. Carefully lift them onto the baking sheet, leaving a little space between each strip. Brush remaining egg onto the galletas.

Bake in oven for 10 to 15 minutes until golden brown.

Remove from oven and allow to cool slightly. Using a long spatula, transfer the galletas to a wire rack to cool completely.

If any are left after tasting, store them in an airtight container at room temperature.

Sea Salt and Olive Oil Crackers

These crackers came about while I was cooking for clients on location, far from a store. I had bought the cheese but forgot the crackers! I had to think on my feet and throw something together quickly. I came up with these flaky, rich-flavored crackers that are not complicated to make and also table-ready within an hour. SERVES 8-10

what you need

2 cups all-purpose flour,
   plus more for rolling dough

1 teaspoon baking soda

1 teaspoon of *A Taste of Ojai Culinary Sea Salts (Lavender, Wild Fennel, or Pink Pepper)* or your favorite sea salt,
   plus extra for sprinkling

1 cup water

¼ cup extra-virgin olive oil,
   plus ¼ cup for brushing

how to make it

Preheat oven to 425°F and line 2 baking sheets with parchment.

In a large bowl stir together the flour, baking soda, and flavored sea salt.

Make a little well in the middle of the flour and pour in half the water with ¼ cup of olive oil. With a wooden spoon, mix the water into the dry ingredients together, adding a little more water as you go, until it becomes a soft ball. Knead the dough on the counter for a few minutes with a little extra flour to avoid sticking until it becomes a smooth dough ball.

Place dough ball on a floured work surface, split the dough into two pieces and roll each piece until it's ¼ inch thick. Place each on a parchment-lined baking sheet. Brush generously with olive oil, then sprinkle lightly with flavored sea salts.

Bake for 20 minutes then check the color—you want it crisp and golden brown. If it's not, bake for 3 or 4 more minutes, but keep watch since it crisps up and browns quickly. Remove from oven and cool for 10 minutes. Slide these big crackers onto a serving tray or basket. Break into smaller rustic pieces and serve.

Lavender Fig Crackers

These homemade treats are just as good if not better than the expensive variety you find in gourmet food stores. These take a bit of pre-planning and time but well worth the effort. In this recipe, you first make the dough and bake it in loaves, then slice the loaves to make the crackers. Loaded with dried fruits and toasted nuts and seeds, they are delicious to snack on their own or with a spread or cheese plate. MAKES ABOUT 50 CRACKERS

what you need

Olive oil or cooking spray

½ cup walnuts or pistachios
   or both, chopped

¼ cup pepitas (pumpkin seeds)

1½ cups all-purpose flour

½ cup whole-wheat flour

2 teaspoons baking soda

1½ teaspoons sea salt

¼ cup light honey

2 cups plain yogurt

1 cup dried figs (or dried apricots
   or currants), chopped

¼ cup sunflower seeds, shelled

¼ cup sesame seeds

2 teaspoons dried lavender,
   finely chopped

1 teaspoon ground fennel seed

how to make it

Preheat oven 350°F.

Generously grease two 9-by-5-inch loaf pans with olive oil or cooking spray.

Place the nuts and pepitas on a baking sheet and toast in the oven for 10 minutes. Set aside to cool.

In a large bowl, combine the flours, baking soda, and sea salt. Add reserved toasted nuts, dried figs, seeds and stir to combine. In a separate bowl, stir together honey and yogurt with the lavender and fennel and add to dry ingredients and stir with a heavy wooden spoon until just combined.

Divide the batter between the two loaf pans, pressing down lightly into the pan and bake about 35-40 minutes until golden and the top springs back when lightly poked. Remove from the pans and leave to cool. Once fully cooled, wrap them well with foil and place them in the freezer until firm or frozen, which makes it easier to slice.

To toast: Preheat oven to 300°F. With a long serrated bread knife, slice frozen loaves into thin ¼-inch slices and place them in a single layer on a baking sheet. Bake for 10 minutes on one side, flip them over, and then bake for another 10 minutes. If they feel soft, continue to toast at 5-minute intervals until they are crisp, careful not to burn them.

Transfer to a wire rack and cool. Store in an airtight container until ready to serve.

Tip: The crackers may soften after a few days from moisture in the air. To crisp them up, place them in a 250°F oven for 5 to 7 minutes, let them cool, and they will be perfect again.

Index

Index

About the Author

Robin Goldstein is a California chef who works her culinary magic combining unique flavor and spices with local seasonal products, to create an unforgettable culinary experience for the palate and on the plate, in private homes and public venues. Known as "Private Chef Robin" to celebrity and private clients alike, Robin has made a career of providing an intimate home-cooked experience that is anything but traditional home-cooked food. Robin uses classic techniques she honed at the Culinary Institute of America in New York. Through travel and work abroad for many years, she has developed what might be called a Mediterranean cooking style, with an emphasis on Middle Eastern flavors. She also works closely with private clients teaching them how to select ingredients, cook intelligently and live better with healthful options, without sacrificing flavor. Teaching locally at the Lavender Inn in Ojai, CA, Robin develops and fully infuses lavender into recipes that have been featured during the Ojai Lavender Festival for several years. This success has led to recent development of a new product line "A Taste of Ojai Culinary Sea Salts" that infuses lavender, wild fennel and pink peppercorns into three distinct and flavorful seasoning blends. Robin was born and raised in the Washington DC area where she ate her way through the city's most prominent restaurants at a very young age. Her early exposure to fine dining at her grandparents' restaurant and later, her father's restaurant, along with her food-loving family sparked her lifelong passion and love of cooking. Robin lives in an oak shaded neighborhood in the Ojai Valley, surrounded by nature and the scenic beauty of the local mountains that Ojai is famed for. This first book in a series "A Taste of Ojai – A Collection of Small Plates" shares some of her secrets of creating healthy and delicious fresh fare for her private events, with a dash of Ojai thrown in.

Contributors

Photographer : Karen Nedivi

Karen Nedivi is an Ojai based artist, mother, & aspiring homesteader. She is founder of Hand Eye Pictures, offering services in all things videography and photography. This project combined her passion for photography, food, and collaboration. She lives in Matilija Canyon with her husband, Vaughn, two kids, chickens, puppy and bugs, all of whom challenge and inspire her everyday.

To see more of her work, visit: handeyepictures.com

Publication Design : Tracy Smith

Publication designer and longtime Ojai area resident, Tracy Smith combines all the things she loves right here in the Ojai Valley. "I was thrilled when Robin tapped me to design her new cookbook. She is an inspiring and creative chef and as it turns out, a great photo-food stylist as well! We all had a lot of fun putting this project together and it shows."

To see more of her work, visit: tracysmithstudio.com

Acknowledgement

Above all, I want to thank all my private clients who have inspired me to cook and create these recipes through the years.

I would like to thank Tracy Smith, my designer and art director, for the hours upon hours she has poured into the book, and Karen Nedivi my photographer as well, both for their invaluable time and energy helping through the process of creating my first cookbook. Thanks to Heidi Dvorak, for editing my recipes. All my friends and family for their support and well wishes and encouragement and my kids...who helped eat all the food testing. Hudson-Grace in Montecito, generously allowing me to use some of their table wares for my photo shoots. Karen Scott/Bernscott Pottery, Eilam Byle and Scott Chatenever for their handmade wares. Julie Grist for her help with words and Kristina Kulik for her advice and opinion.

37292760R00065